ROTHERHAM PUBLIC LIBRARIES

This book must be returned by the latest date entered above.
The loan may be extended [personally, by post or telephone]
for a further period if the book is not required by another reader.

LMI

PROJECTS FOR EASTER

Jean Cooke

Illustrated by Janos Marffy

Seasonal Projects
Projects for Spring
Projects for Summer
Projects for Autumn
Projects for Winter
Projects for Christmas
Projects for Easter

First published in 1989 by
Wayland (Publishers) Limited
61 Western Road, Hove
East Sussex BN3 1JD, England

© Copyright 1989 Wayland (Publishers) Ltd

Editor: Jane Edmonds
Designer: Ross George

British Library Cataloguing in Publication Data
Cooke, Jean
    Projects for Easter.
    1. Seasonal activities for children. – For children
    I. Title   II. Marffy, Janos   III. Series
    790.1'922

    ISBN 1–85210–366–3

Typeset by Kalligraphics Ltd, Horley, Surrey
Printed and bound in Italy by Sagdos S.p.A., Milan

Cover/top *A Palm Sunday procession in Jerusalem.*
Cover/below left *Making an Easter bird.*
Cover/below right *Decorated eggs for Easter.*

Contents

THE EASTER SEASON

This Palm Sunday procession in Guatemala, Central America, is one of many processions held by Christians throughout the world during Holy Week. It commemorates Jesus's last journey to Jerusalem.

Easter is the most important festival in the Christian Church. It commemorates the Crucifixion of Jesus and, on the third day, his Resurrection – rising from the dead. It comes at the end of Holy Week, in which Christians remember the events leading up to the Resurrection.

Jesus was put to death just before the Jewish festival of Passover, which happens in the spring. The old European pagan (non-Christian) religions used to have feasts at about the same time to mark the coming of spring. So when Christian missionaries were converting the pagans they linked the two festivals to encourage the pagans to adopt the new religion.

In many languages Easter has names that come from *Pesach*, the Hebrew name for Passover. They include the French *Pâques*, the Spanish *Pascua* and the Italian *Pasqua*. The English name probably comes from that of the old Anglo-Saxon goddess of spring, Eostre. The German names, *das Ostern* or *das Osterfest*, have the same origin.

Easter Sunday does not come on exactly the same day each year, but it always comes between 22 March and 25 April. The day is fixed by taking the first Sunday that follows the first full moon after 21 March. This is because the date of Passover is based on the Hebrew calendar in which the months are *lunar months*, that is, months based on the phases of the moon.

EASTER DAY	
Here are the dates of Easter until the year 2000, the end of the twentieth century:	
1989	26 March
1990	15 April
1991	31 March
1992	19 April
1993	11 April
1994	3 April
1995	16 April
1996	7 April
1997	30 March
1998	12 April
1999	4 April
2000	23 April

EASTER CARDS

One of the ways in which people celebrate Easter is to give each other Easter cards. The cards are often decorated with a picture of an egg, a chicken, a hare or a rabbit. You will find out why these pictures are symbols of Easter later in this book.

To make a simple Easter card you will need:

- **a thick sheet of A4 paper in any cheerful colour**
- **a sheet of A4 paper in a contrasting colour**
- **tracing paper**
- **scissors**
- **glue**

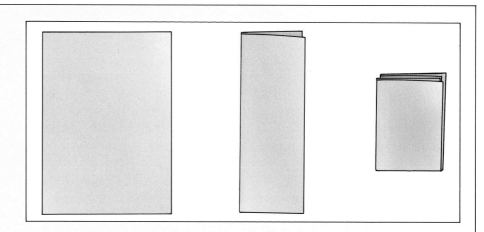

1 Fold the thick sheet of paper lengthways, then in half again.

2 Find a picture that is a symbol of Easter, in a book or magazine. Trace the outline on some tracing paper.

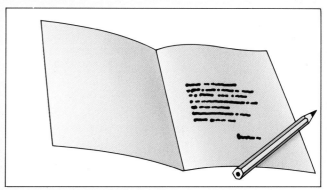

3 Trace the outline on to the second sheet of coloured paper and cut it out.

4 Stick this cut-out on the front of your folded card. Print the words 'HAPPY EASTER' across the top.

5 On the inside you can write a message or perhaps a little poem.

PALM SUNDAY

Palm Sunday is the Sunday before Easter Day. It commemorates Jesus's last journey to Jerusalem, when his supporters cut palm branches to spread in his path as he rode to the city. At that time Jerusalem was ruled by the Romans, and it was a Roman custom to strew palm leaves in front of a hero. Among the ordinary people of Jerusalem, Jesus was a popular hero of the day.

From the earliest days of Christianity people have celebrated Palm Sunday by gathering palm leaves. In places where palms do not grow they gather green leaves and twigs from other trees.

The greenery is used to decorate the churches. For hundreds of years people used to gather in one church, where the palms were blessed, and then walk in procession to another church to hear Mass (the ceremony of Holy Communion). In the Greek Orthodox Church and most Protestant Churches there is no procession, though some do use palm leaves. Ukrainian Christians of the Russian Orthodox Church use willow branches, and call the day 'Willow Sunday'. Priests in the Coptic Church of Egypt give children palm leaves blessed and sprinkled with holy water. The children keep the leaves for a whole year.

Many other traditions are associated with Palm Sunday. In some parts of England it used to be called Fig Sunday because people ate fig pies or puddings on that day. In Wales it is still called *Sul y Blodau*, Flowering Sunday, because of an old custom of decorating family graves with flowers.

In Greece people like to eat fish on Palm Sunday. In some German towns people decorate poles with streamers and branches of pussy willow. Christians in Lebanon like to wear new clothes on Palm Sunday. In Italy it is regarded as a day for making up quarrels.

SWEDISH DECORATION

In Sweden children decorate branches with coloured feathers tied on with thread or wire.

You will need:
- **branches with buds or green leaves, such as birch or pussy willow**
- **feathers**
- **coloured inks**
- **fine wire or strong thread**

1 Dip the feathers in the coloured inks and spread them out to dry.

2 Tie the feathers to the branches using the thread or wire.

3 Arrange the branches in a vase of water. The buds will then open.

DUTCH PALMPAAS

In the Netherlands children decorate a stick, the palmpaas, and carry it round the farms, collecting eggs.

You will need:

- a wire coat hanger
- a length of cane about 60 cm long
- fine wire or strong thread
- coloured ribbons
- spring flowers and leaves
- an orange
- plasticine

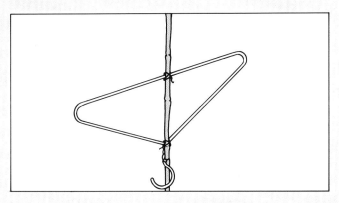

1 With wire or thread, tie the coat hanger upside down to the cane, about 10 cm from the top. This will give you the shape of a cross.

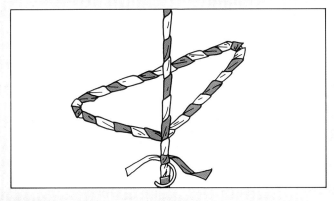

2 Cover the cane and coat hanger by winding coloured ribbons around them.

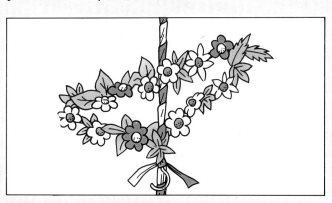

3 Use thread to bind the flowers and leaves to the hanger.

4 Put a particularly large flower or orange on the hook of the hanger.

5 Dutch children shape a cockerel or Easter hare in dough and push it on to the top of the cane. You could make one out of plasticine.

EASTER EGGS

For Christians, the egg is a symbol of Jesus's Resurrection. It is an Easter custom, particularly in Eastern Europe, to paint eggs with elaborate designs.

For thousands of years, people have thought of eggs as the symbols of new life because they have seen birds hatching from eggs. People very long ago even thought that the Earth itself hatched from a huge egg. So naturally enough, the early Christians chose the egg as a symbol of the Resurrection. As a result, eggs have always been a part of the Easter celebrations.

Long before the days of Jesus, people used to give each other eggs as presents in spring. They dyed or painted them in fancy colours. And today we colour our Easter eggs, too.

Some of the most beautiful and elaborate designs for Easter eggs come from countries in Eastern Europe, and especially from the Ukraine, which is part of the USSR. Even those Americans whose ancestors were Ukrainians keep up the old customs.

The tool the Ukrainians use is called a *kistka*. It is a little brass cone mounted on a stick. The artist fills the cone with wax and heats it so that the wax melts. Then the artist draws patterns on the egg with melted wax. The wax protects the shell against the dyes that will form the final design.

The artist either dips the egg in the dye, or paints it on with a brush, starting with the lightest colour – usually yellow – first. After the first colour has dried the artist draws more lines over it with wax and adds more dye. When the pattern is complete the egg is warmed to melt the wax, revealing the full beauty of the egg. A coat of varnish protects the design.

All the designs used have a religious meaning. For example, the cross is a symbol of Jesus's death on a cross and the fish is an ancient symbol of Christianity.

DECORATED EGGS

You can make decorated eggs with both simple and complicated designs.

You will need:
- **white-shelled eggs**
- **a choice of onion skins, beetroot, spinach or food dyes**
- **sheets of paper**
- **scissors**
- **coloured inks or felt-tip pens**
- **paraffin wax**
- **a stiff paintbrush**
- **a large needle**

1 You can dye an egg a single colour by hard-boiling it with one of the following:

  onion skins for golden yellow
beetroot for red
spinach leaves for green
a few drops of food dye

Try tying an onion skin or spinach leaf round the egg before you boil it to make a more interesting pattern.

2 When the boiled egg is dry you can paint patterns on it. Use paper and scissors to make a stencil of a pattern you like. Wrap it round the egg and dab dye or coloured ink through the holes.

As an egg is head-shaped, try drawing a face on it.

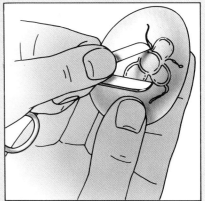

3 Dip a hard-boiled egg in paraffin wax and then scratch your pattern right through to the shell.
Dip the egg in cold dye.

The dye will only stick where there is no wax. When it is dry, put the egg in a warm oven on a piece of paper towel, so that the wax can melt off.

EASTER EGG CUSTOMS

Wherever people celebrate Easter, they have Easter eggs. Every country has its own customs, some of them very old indeed. In the northern counties of England children go round 'Pace egging', begging for eggs and other presents, and acting the Pace egg play. This is one of the Mumming plays, performed at Christmas and other seasons for hundreds of years. The Pace egg play includes such characters as Old Betsy Brownbags and Jolly Jack Tar.

'Pace eggs' is another name for Pasch or Easter eggs, and comes from the Hebrew word *Pesach* (Passover). In Scotland the same word also appears as Peace or Paiss.

Egg rolling is an old Easter pastime still followed in parts of Britain. Many people roll eggs just for the fun of it, but in Germany it becomes a competition, known as *Eierlesen*. The winner receives a prize of 101 eggs.

Children gather every Easter Monday on the lawn of the White House to roll eggs.

It is now a custom throughout the Christian world to exchange chocolate eggs on Easter Sunday. They are often decorated with swirls of icing and chocolate patterns.

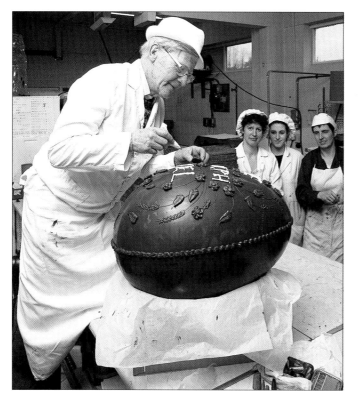

In the USA thousands of children gather every Easter Monday on the lawn of the White House in Washington, DC, to roll decorated, hard-boiled eggs down a slope. Children also run egg and spoon races in Central Park, New York City.

In Poland girls used to send decorated eggs to their favourite boyfriends. Finnish children beat the grown-ups with birch twigs on Easter Day until they are given a ransom of Easter eggs.

In countries of south-eastern Europe people dye hard-boiled eggs red. Greeks and Romanians carry scarlet eggs on Easter Day. When friends meet they tap their eggs together with the greeting, 'Christ is risen', to which the reply is, 'Truly he is risen'. Some East Europeans bury a scarlet egg in a family grave as a symbol of the Resurrection, while in the Balkans scarlet eggs are buried in the fields to make the crops grow well.

CHOCOLATE EGGS

Chocolate eggs, now a world-wide favourite, were first introduced in France, Italy, the Netherlands and Spain about 150 years ago. You can make your own chocolate egg.

You will need:

- a large egg
- a needle
- 100 g plain or milk chocolate
- an egg cup
- a small jug
- sugar flowers or white icing

1 Use the needle to make a fairly big hole in the top of the egg. Shake out the yolk and white into a bowl to cook later.

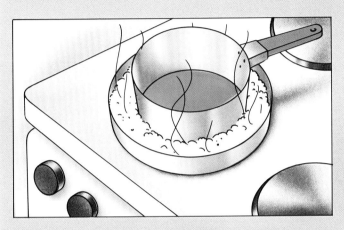

2 Melt the chocolate in a small pan set in a larger pan of boiling water. Pour the melted chocolate into the jug.

3 When the emptied egg has dried out, support it in an egg cup and pour the melted chocolate through the hole.

4 Leave the egg in a cool place to harden, then break open the shell.

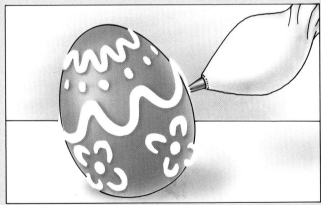

5 You can decorate the chocolate egg with sugar flowers stuck on with more melted chocolate, or with swirls of white icing squeezed through an icing nozzle.

EASTER CAROLS AND DANCES

Carols used to be sung at Easter as well as Christmas and we think that people sometimes danced to their tunes. The word carol originally meant a 'ring dance', so if you write an Easter carol (see below), try making up the steps of a ring dance to go with the music.

If you thought that carols were sung only at Christmas, you would be wrong. When they were most popular – in the 1400s to the mid-1600s – they were sung at all times of the year. Many of the older carols, especially those from continental European countries, were written to be sung at Easter or in spring. Because people in the 1800s thought about carols only at Christmas, some of the best spring carols had new words put to the fine old tunes.

One of the jolliest of these old tunes was printed in 1582. Its words were in Latin, and began *Tempus adest floridum* which can be translated as 'Spring has now brought forth the flowers'. You probably do not know the words but you will have sung the tune many times, to the words of 'Good King Wenceslas'!

One old French carol designed especially for Easter has words which begin (as translated) 'Cheer up, friends and neighbours, now it's Easter tide.' Another Easter carol has the title 'Easter eggs', and was a traditional Russian song. You will find many others in your carol books.

The word 'carol' originally meant a ring dance, and we think that people at one time used to dance as well as sing to carol tunes. Certainly some of the old tunes are very dance-like and lively.

WRITE A CAROL

Choose a well-known carol tune that you usually sing at Christmas and write the words of an Easter carol of your own that will fit the rhythm.

LOVE IS COME AGAIN

NOW THE GREEN BLADE RI — SETH FROM THE BU — RIED GRAIN,

WHEAT THAT IN DARK EARTH MA — NY DAYS HAS LAIN;

MAKE A MOBILE

Try making a mobile to illustrate the words of your carol. If you do not think there are enough words that you can illustrate, make a mobile of some Easter symbols.

You will need:
- **a sheet of thin cardboard**
- **felt-tip pens or paints**
- **strong thread**
- **lengths of fine cane**
- **a needle**

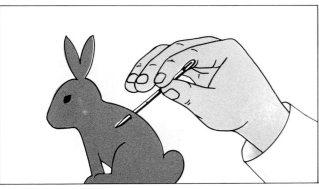

1 On the cardboard, draw the objects you have decided to include in your mobile.

2 Colour them in on both sides with felt-tip pens or paints, then cut them out.

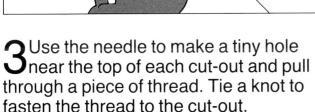

3 Use the needle to make a tiny hole near the top of each cut-out and pull through a piece of thread. Tie a knot to fasten the thread to the cut-out.

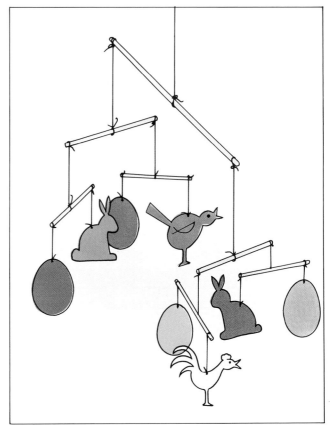

4 Hang your cut-outs from lengths of fine cane so that they balance.

EASTER GAMES

Because Easter, with its message of hope for mankind, has always been a time of rejoicing for Christians everywhere, it has also been the custom for people to play lively games at this time of the year.

In parts of southern England the marbles season ran from Ash Wednesday (the beginning of the period of fasting and repentance called Lent) to noon on Good Friday, which was often called Marble Day.

In England Easter Monday is still sometimes referred to as 'Ball Monday' because of the many ball games that used to be played on that day. They included such traditional games as stoolball, knurr and spell, trapball, ninepins and handball. Football is still a regular Easter Monday game.

Football is regularly played on Easter Monday, a day which in England is still sometimes called 'Ball Monday'.

When settlers from Europe emigrated to America they took their customs and their sports with them. The Dutch, for example, took their traditional game of ninepin bowling. But people used to gamble so much on this game that the state of Connecticut banned it. So the ingenious bowlers added a tenth pin, and that was the origin of the popular American sport of tenpin bowling.

It is interesting that many games that are now played only by children, such as tipcat and prisoners' base, used to be played by grown-ups, and were among the Easter sports.

NINE MEN'S MORRIS

One of the oldest traditional games of Europe is called Nine Men's Morris. It's very easy to make and to play.

You will need:
- a piece of card about 30 cm square
- 18 small pieces of wood
- black and white paint

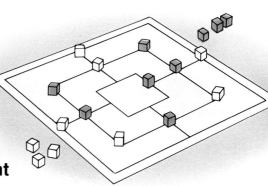

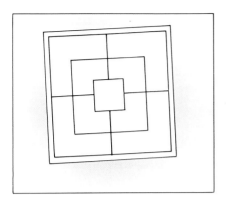

1 Make the board from the piece of card. Mark it out as shown in the diagram.

2 To make the counters – or men – paint nine of the pieces of wood white and the other nine black.

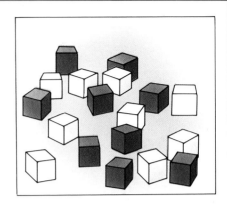

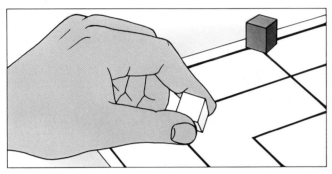

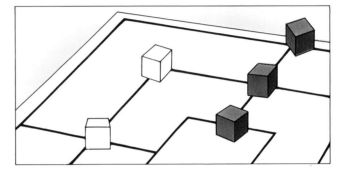

3 To play the game, you will have all the white counters or all the black counters and your opponent will have the other colour. Begin by taking it in turns to place one man on the board at any point where lines meet.

4 Try to get three men along a straight line to form a 'mill'. Once you have a mill you can 'pound' your opponent by removing one of his or her men. This man should not be part of a mill unless there is no other man available.

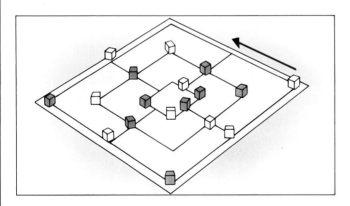

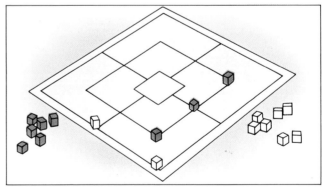

5 When all the men are on the board you can take turns to move them along the lines to try to form new mills. Every time you form a new mill you can take one of your opponent's men.

6 The game ends when one player has only two men left or is unable to move.

MAUNDY THURSDAY

A Greek Orthodox priest pours out water in preparation for the maundy foot-washing ceremony. The ceremony is held in memory of Jesus's act of washing his disciples' feet at the Last Supper.

The word 'maundy' comes from the Latin version of St John's Gospel, Chapter 13, verse 34: *Mandatum novum do vobis* ('A new commandment I give unto you'), and it means 'commandment'. These words were spoken by Jesus after he had washed his disciples' feet at the Last Supper. For hundreds of years many Christian monarchs in Europe used to wash the feet of poor people on the Thursday before Easter in memory of Jesus's act. The foot washing tradition continues in Roman Catholic churches. In Rome, the Pope washes the feet of thirteen priests at a ceremony in St Peter's Basilica.

In other churches the priests wash the feet of twelve poor people of the parish in front of the altar of their church during the evening celebration of Mass. There are similar foot-washing ceremonies in Eastern Orthodox churches.

Other names for Maundy Thursday are Holy Thursday, in most European countries; Sheer Thursday, meaning 'Clean Thursday', in England; and *Gründonnerstag*, meaning Green Thursday, in German-speaking lands. This last name recalls an old custom of giving people a green branch as a token that the fast of Lent was over. It is thought to be unlucky if you do not eat some green food on that day.

A MAUNDY PURSE

In Britain today, one old man and one old woman for each year of the Queen's age take part in a special maundy ceremony. In this ceremony the Queen gives them coloured leather purses containing specially minted coins. You can make your own maundy purse.

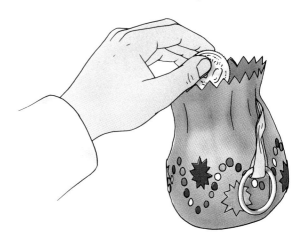

You will need:

- **two pieces of felt or soft leather, 10 cm by 30 cm and 2 cm by 18 cm**
- **a curtain ring**
- **needle and thread**
- **scissors and pinking shears**

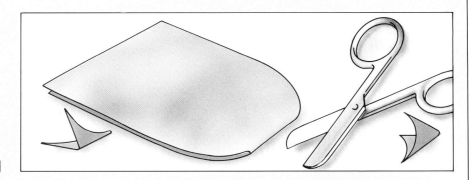

1 Fold the larger piece of fabric in half, right sides together, and round off the lower corners with the scissors.

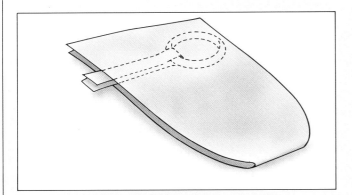

2 Fold the smaller piece around the curtain ring and insert the ends into one side seam of the purse. The ring and loop will now be inside with only the ends of the loop showing outside.

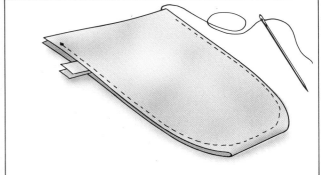

3 Stitch round the purse, sewing in the ring loop as you go. Do not sew along the top. Instead, leave it open and trim with pinking shears.

4 Turn the purse right side out. Gather the top of the purse together and slip over the ring.

5 If you are using felt, you may like to decorate your purse by gluing on scraps of felt, or sequins.

GOOD FRIDAY

A stained glass window in a fifteenth-century church depicts the Crucifixion of Jesus, an event which is commemorated on Good Friday.

Good Friday is the commemoration of the trial and Crucifixion of Jesus. In many churches the altars are draped in purple on that day as a sign of mourning. Some Christians keep the day as one of fasting and prayer. Special services are held in the afternoon, centred on three o'clock, because this is the biblical ninth hour at which Jesus died. Religious processions are held in many Roman Catholic and Orthodox communities, such as those of Malta, Greece and Italy. In Greece the church

bells are tolled solemnly on Good Friday, but in France and some other European countries they are silenced on that day until Sunday. Children are told that the bells have gone to Rome to bring back their Easter eggs.

A custom that started in England, and has since spread to other countries, is the eating of hot cross buns. Like many other customs, this one is based on a pre-Christian tradition. The ancient Greeks used to offer their gods a cake symbolizing a bull, with a cross for its horns.

Many superstitions go with hot cross buns. They are said to be a charm against evil and to keep indefinitely. An old rhyme says:

Good Friday comes this month: the old woman runs
With one a penny, two a penny hot cross buns;
Whose virtue is, if you'll believe what's said,
They'll not grow mouldy like the common bread.

Other customs include burning an effigy of Judas, the disciple who betrayed Jesus, in Portugal, Sicily and Spain.

STAINED GLASS WINDOWS

In many churches you will find stained glass windows showing the events which led up to the Crucifixion. You can make your own simple version of a stained glass window.

You will need:
- **a piece of thick card**
- **pieces of blue, red, yellow, green and purple cellophane**
- **scissors**
- **adhesive paste**
- **thick thread**

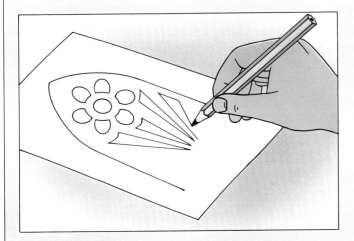

1 Work out the design for your window on a piece of paper, then draw it on to the piece of card.

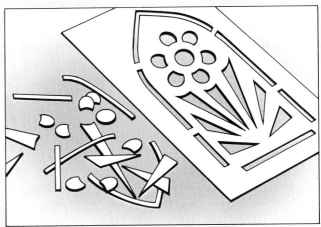

2 Cut out parts of the design so that you are left with a card framework.

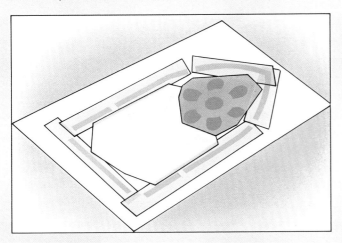

3 Paste pieces of cellophane across the back of the window to look like glass.

4 Hang it by a thread in front of a real window so that the light shines through it.

HOLY SATURDAY

Churches are brilliantly lit with candles at midnight on Holy Saturday. This is the beginning of a joyful day for Christians when the Resurrection of Jesus is commemorated.

The day between Good Friday and Easter Day is the last day of Lent, the forty-day fast which precedes Easter. It is known in the Christian world as Holy Saturday or Easter Saturday.

It is a day of waiting in the Christian Churches, as it was for Jesus's sorrowing followers after the Crucifixion. That day was also the Jewish Sabbath, which still officially begins at sundown on Friday and lasts until Saturday. In the year of the Crucifixion it was also the first day of Passover, which lasts for a week. The body of Jesus was laid in a tomb before the Sabbath began.

In Roman Catholic countries generally, Holy Saturday is part of the period of mourning which begins on Good Friday. The ceremony of burning an effigy of Judas, which is kept on Good Friday in many European countries, is observed on Holy Saturday in some countries of Latin America.

In European countries bonfires used to be lit on Easter eve. This was probably associated in people's minds with the ceremonies in their churches, where the candles which were put out as a sign of mourning on Good Friday were relit. For Christians in countries such as Bulgaria, Greece and Poland, Holy Saturday is a day of cooking, ready for the feasting the following day to celebrate the Resurrection.

At midnight on Holy Saturday the first service of Easter Day begins, with the church brilliantly lit with candles in token of the Resurrection.

DECORATE A SIMNEL CAKE

Some people bake simnel cake, ready for Sunday. You can decorate a simnel cake with marzipan.

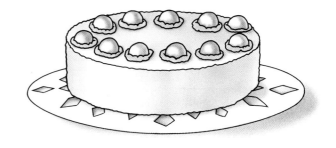

You will need:
- a simnel cake
- apricot jam
- ready-made marzipan

or
- 125 g caster sugar
- 125 g ground almonds
- a small egg

1 To make your own marzipan, beat the egg and then mix it with the sugar and almonds. If the mixture is too soft, add some icing sugar.

2 Roll the marzipan into eleven balls – that's one for each of Jesus's disciples, but not including Judas the betrayer.

3 Put eleven little blobs of apricot jam around the edge of the cake to hold the marzipan, then push the 'disciples' firmly in place.

MAKE A DOILY

You can show off your decorated simnel cake by placing it on a doily.

You will need:
- a piece of thin white paper
- scissors
- a plate

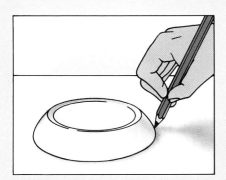

1 Draw a circle on the paper round the edge of a plate turned upside down and cut it out.

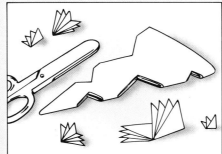

2 Fold the paper in half three or four times and snip out little triangles along the two folded edges.

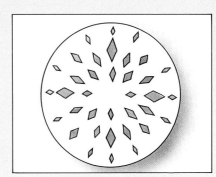

3 Open out the paper and you will find an all-over pattern.

EASTER DAY

Easter Day, or Easter Sunday, is the most joyful day of the Christian year because it commemorates the Resurrection of Jesus, with its promise of eternal life.

Celebrations start for many people at dawn. It was an ancient tradition in Britain to climb the nearest hill to see the sun rise, because people believed it danced for joy on that morning. This dawn tradition is still carried on in some parts of the world: for example Americans attend outdoor services at dawn in such places as the Hollywood Bowl, a huge open-air theatre in California.

In the churches, which were draped in purple on Good Friday, all is now white and bright again. The bells ring out for the Easter morning service. On this day it was customary for people to wear new clothes, and this idea has been carried on to the modern 'Easter parade', with its Easter bonnets or smart hats.

There is always a feast. Various foods are popular in different places – for example, hot cross buns in Australia (rather than on Friday); simnel

Easter bonnets for an Easter Day parade.

cake in Britain (it used to be eaten on Mothering Sunday in mid-lent); *pacoca*, a paste containing crushed nuts, in Brazil; Easter cakes in Finland and Italy; turkey or chicken in Lebanon; and *pasenbrood*, a sweet loaf containing raisins and currants, in the Netherlands. Above all, Easter Day is the time for Easter eggs.

EASTER BONNET

You might like to wear the sort of bonnet traditionally worn on Easter Sunday.

You will need:
- **a piece of firm fabric or stiff paper, such as wallpaper**
- **scissors**
- **needle and thread or glue**
- **a length of ribbon**

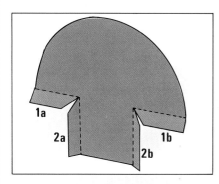

1 Cut the shape of the pattern out of your piece of material or paper.

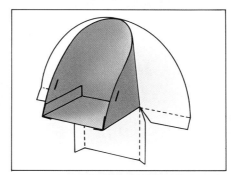

2 Cut the two slots. Then sew or stick flap 1a to flap 2a and flap 1b to flap 2b.

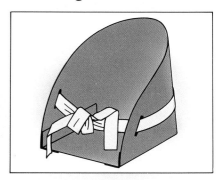

3 Thread the length of ribbon through the slots and tie the bonnet under your chin.

MA'AMOUL

Today is a good time to entertain your friends. Make them a batch of ma'amoul, an Easter speciality from the Lebanon filled with dates or nuts.

You will need:
- **300 g flour**
- **150 g butter**
- **two tablespoonfuls of milk**
- **a few drops of rose water, or more milk**
- **300 g stoneless dates**
- **crushed nuts**
- **sugar and cinnamon**
- **icing sugar**

  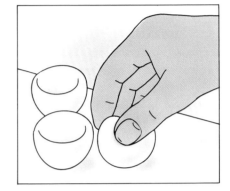

1 Make the pastry by rubbing the flour and butter together in a big bowl, and then add the milk and rose water to make a soft dough.

2 Chop up the dates and put them in a pan with six tablespoonfuls of water over a low heat until they go soft and squishy.

3 Roll a small lump of pastry into a ball, then press your thumb in it to make a little pot. Repeat this until you have several little pots.

4 Fill some pots with the date mixture and the others with the crushed nuts mixed with sugar and cinnamon. For each pot, press the edges of the pastry together.

5 Put all the filled pots on a baking tray and cook them for about 25 minutes at gas mark 4, electric 350°F (180°C), but do not let them turn brown. When they are cool, roll them in icing sugar.

EASTER MONDAY

The Easter bunny is a traditional part of Easter, especially in the USA.

The Monday after Easter Day is a holiday in many countries. It has always been a day for sports and games of various kinds. In Britain football is the most popular sport today, but in times past plenty of other games were played, including many games with Easter eggs.

One widely played Easter Monday egg game in Britain and other European countries was egg shackling, in which you hold a hard-boiled egg firmly in your hand and strike it against one held by your opponent.

Another popular sport has given Easter Monday its alternative name of Ducking Monday. In Poland boys and girls splash each other with water. In Hungary the girls only are soaked.

Monday is also associated with the legend of the Easter hare, though this mythical animal is also remembered on other days. The hare was sacred to the pagan goddess Eostre, and the legend goes back long before Christianity began. By tradition in many countries the Easter hare brings children their Easter eggs.

AN EASTER BUNNY

In the USA, where hares are often called rabbits, the Easter hare has become the Easter bunny. Make an Easter bunny from any marzipan left over after you decorated the simnel cake on Saturday.

You will need:
- **marzipan**
- **silver or gold confectionery beads**

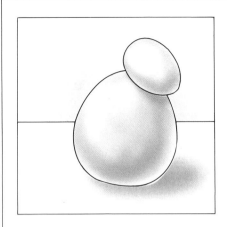

1 Roll a round lump of marzipan for the body and stick on a smaller lump for the head.

2 Roll out two little sausage-shaped pieces, flatten them for ears, and place them on the head. Add a small round nose to the face and a little lump to the back of the body to make the tail.

3 Use the confectionery beads for the eyes.

AN EGG COSY

You can make an egg cosy that looks like an Easter bunny.

You will need:
- **a piece of felt**
- **a needle and thread**
- **scissors**
- **cotton wool**
- **glue**
- **a felt-tip pen**

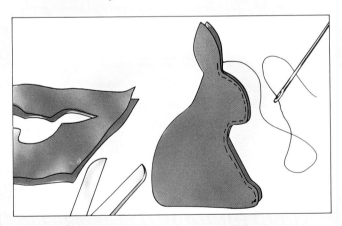

1 Cut two pieces of felt in the shape of a bunny and sew them together with blanket stitch.

2 Draw in the eyes with the felt-tip pen, then stick a fluffy piece of cotton wool at the back for a tail.

OTHER EASTER DAYS

This nineteenth-century illustration shows the old Easter custom of 'lifting' which was supposed to bring good luck. In places where the women were lifted on Easter Monday, the men were lifted on the Tuesday, and vice-versa.

Eastertide goes on until Whit Sunday, fifty days after Easter Day. Whitsun is short for 'White Sunday', because on that day people who were newly baptized wore their white robes in procession. The day is also known as Pentecost, from a Greek word meaning fifty. On that day Jesus's followers received the Holy Spirit, which gave them renewed courage to go forth into the world and preach his gospel.

Several other days during Eastertide have special traditions attached to them. The first Sunday after Easter is known as Low Sunday. It is also called Quasimodo Sunday because in Latin the Mass said on that day begins with the words *Quasi modo geniti infantes*, 'As newborn babes'.

In England the Monday and Tuesday following Low Sunday are called Hocktide. On Hock Monday the women of a village used to go out with ropes to catch and bind any men they could, releasing them only on payment of a ransom. On Hock Tuesday the men did the same to the women. The money generally went towards church funds. The Hocktide tradition is at least a thousand years old.

AN EGG TREE

Something you can do in the Easter holiday is make an egg tree to display eggs you have blown and decorated.

You will need:
- **eggs (which are at room temperature)**
- **a needle and thread**
- **a leafless branch**
- **caster sugar**
- **paints or coloured inks**
- **a stiff brush**
- **matchsticks**

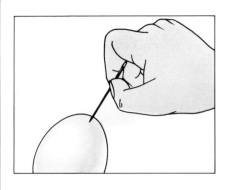

1 To blow an egg, first use the needle to make a tiny hole in the smaller end of the egg. Make a larger hole in the other end.

2 Cover each hole with a finger and shake the egg hard to break the yolk.

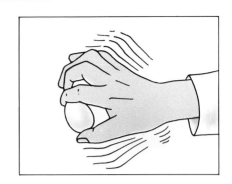

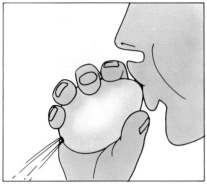

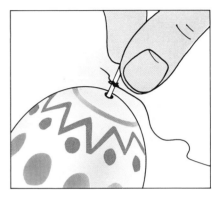

3 Hold the egg over a bowl and blow through the smaller of the two holes. Continue blowing until the egg is empty. Then leave it to dry.

4 Decorate your blown eggs using the stiff brush and paints or coloured inks.

5 Attach a length of thread to each egg by tying the thread to a piece of matchstick. Push this through the bigger hole in the egg.

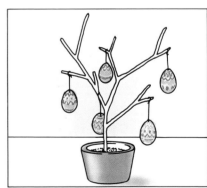

6 To make your egg tree, either paint the branch or sugar-frost it. To sugar-frost it, whisk one egg white with two teaspoonfuls of water.

7 Paint this mixture evenly on to the branch, then sprinkle it with caster sugar.

8 When the branch is dry, stand it in a tub of sand. Hang the eggs from your tree, like decorations on a Christmas tree.

ASCENSION

Although Eastertide officially lasts until Whitsun, the end of Jesus's life on Earth is marked by Ascension Day, the fortieth day from Easter Day. The New Testament relates that on that day he ascended into Heaven.

Ascension Day falls on a Thursday, and is celebrated as a holy day in Anglican, Eastern Orthodox and Roman Catholic Churches. The Paschal candle, lit on Easter Day to mark the Resurrection, is put out to mark Jesus's departure from Earth.

The Sunday before Ascension is known as Rogation Sunday, and the Monday, Tuesday and Wednesday as the Rogation Days. The name 'Rogation' comes from the Latin word *rogare*, meaning to supplicate, or request humbly. On those days people used to walk in procession, chanting supplications to the saints. Rogation rituals date from AD 470, and are still observed worldwide in the Roman Catholic Church.

One Rogationtide ceremony still observed in many parts of England is that of beating the bounds (in Scotland, riding the marches). The custom grew up at a time when few people could read and there were even fewer maps. To make sure that the boundaries of a parish were clearly marked and remembered, the clergy and parish officers would walk round the boundaries, accompanied by a horde of children. Boys struck the boundary markers with willow wands.

AN EASTER BIRD

Ascension Day marks the end of Jesus's second life on Earth, a life which began with the Resurrection.
As you know, a symbol of the Resurrection is the egg, out of which hatches a bird. You can make an Easter bird using yellow wool.

You will need:

- **a piece of card about 12 cm by 16 cm**
- **a small ball of yellow wool**
- **a large needle**
- **scissors**
- **rubberized glue**
- **a pipecleaner**
- **pieces of felt**
- **thread**

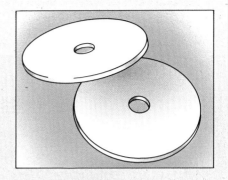

1 Cut two circles of card exactly the same size, about 8 cm across, with a 1·5 cm hole in the middle.

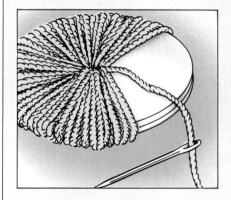

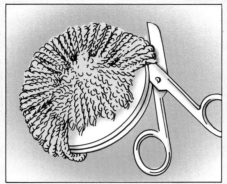

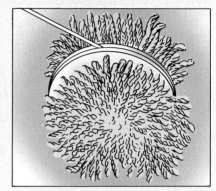

2 Wind the wool round and round both circles until it is quite thick and the hole is filled up. To finish doing this, you will need to thread the wool on a needle.

3 Cut through the wool round the edge to separate the pieces of card.

4 Wind some thread a few times round the bunch of wool between the two pieces of card, and tie a knot. Wind a pipecleaner around the centre.

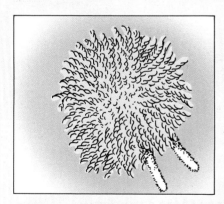

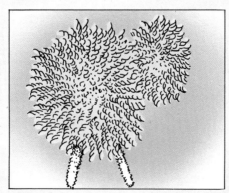

5 Remove the card and you will find you have made a fluffy ball – the body of your bird.

6 Make another, smaller, ball for the head, using circles about 4 cm across. Stick the two balls together with glue.

7 Bend the ends of the pipecleaner to form feet. Make the eyes and beak from felt and glue on.

Glossary

Altar   A table in a church or temple used for the celebration of religious rites.

Anglo-Saxons   Germanic settlers in England in the fifth and sixth centuries.

Ascension   Literally 'going up'; Jesus's going up from Earth to Heaven.

Ash Wednesday   The first day of Lent; so called because it was customary to sprinkle ashes on the head as a sign of mourning.

Balkans   The countries of south-eastern Europe.

Carols   Christian songs of joy or praise, most often sung at Christmas.

Christian   A follower of Christ, the title given to Jesus by his supporters; it means 'saviour'.

Church   With a capital C, means a group of people who worship in the same way; with a small c, a building where they worship.

Coptic Church   The Christian Church in Egypt; Copt means Egyptian.

Disciples   Followers of Jesus.

Easter hare   An imaginary animal said to bring Easter eggs to children.

Egg shackling   A game in which people bang hard-boiled eggs together.

Eostre   The Anglo-Saxon goddess of spring.

Good Friday   The Friday before Easter Day, on which Christians remember Jesus's death.

Gospel   Jesus's teaching, and also any of the New Testament books of Matthew, Mark, Luke and John which tell the story of his life.

Hebrew   The language of the Jews, now one of the official languages of Israel.

Hocktide   The second Monday and Tuesday after Easter.

Holy Week   The week before Easter.

Hot cross bun   A spiced bun marked with a cross, traditionally eaten on Good Friday.

Jerusalem   The ancient capital of the Jews (now capital of Israel), where Jesus was executed.

Jesus   The Greek form of the Hebrew name Joshua; a carpenter's son who lived from about 4 BC to AD 29, believed by Christians to be the Son of God.

Judas   Judas Iscariot, one of Jesus's followers, who betrayed him in return for a bribe of thirty pieces of silver.

Latin   The language of the ancient Romans.

Lent   A period of fasting, from Ash Wednesday to Easter, commemorating Jesus's fast in the wilderness.

Low Sunday   The first Sunday after Easter Day.

Mass   Eating bread and drinking wine as tokens of the flesh and blood of Jesus which he sacrificed to save the rest of mankind.

Maundy Thursday   The Thursday before Easter, on which Christians remember Jesus's washing of his disciples' feet.

Moon, phases of the   The changes in the appearance of the moon caused by the way it is obscured by the Earth's shadow.

Mumming play   An ancient folk play which probably celebrates the death of the year and its resurrection in spring; mummer is an old word for actor.

Orthodox Churches, Eastern   The Christian Churches of eastern Europe and western Asia, including the Greek and Russian Orthodox Churches. They broke away from the main Christian Church in 1045.

Palm Sunday   The Sunday before Easter.

Paschal lamb   The lamb that the Jews used to sacrifice at Passover (Hebrew *Pesach*).

Passover   An annual Jewish feast remembering the Angel of Death passing over the houses of the Jews when he destroyed the first-born of Egypt (see Exodus XII 21–24).

Pentecost   A Jewish feast held fifty days after Passover, from the Greek word for fifty.

Pope   The head of the Roman Catholic Church.

Protestant Churches   Any of the Churches that broke away from the Roman Catholic Church in protest against some of its ways of worship.

Resurrection   Jesus's rising from the dead.

Ring dance   Any dance in which the dancers form a circle.

Rogation Days   The three days before Ascension.

Rogationtide   The three Rogation Days plus the Sunday before.

Roman Catholic Church   The oldest of the Christian Churches, with its headquarters in Rome.

Romans The ancient people of Italy, who created a huge empire in Europe and the Middle East.

Sabbath The weekly day of rest; kept by Jews on Saturday and by Christians on Sunday.

St Peter's Basilica The main church in Rome.

Ukraine One of the 15 republics of the USSR.

White House The official home of the President of the USA.

Whit Sunday Originally 'White Sunday', the seventh Sunday after Easter, the Christian commemoration of Pentecost.

Books to read

Margaret Baker, *Folklore and Customs of Rural England* (David and Charles, 1974)

Norma Fairbairn and Jack Priestley, *Easter* (Religious and Moral Educational Press, 1982)

J. Fox, *Easter* (Wayland, 1984)

Jean Harroven, *Origins of Festivals and Feasts* (Kaye and Ward, 1980)

Christina Hole, *Easter and its Customs* (Bell, 1961)

Christina Hole, *British Folk Customs* (Hutchinson, 1976)

N. Martin, *Christianity* (Wayland, 1985)

Joan Sabin, *Customs and Traditions* (Blackwell, 1973)

Cavell Zangalis and Priscilla Clarke, *Easter for Children* (Hodja Educational Resources Co-operative, 1983)

New English Bible, The New Testament
The Oxford Book of Carols

Picture acknowledgements

Barnaby's Picture Library 4, 18, 28 (top); J. Allan Cash 12, 14, 16; Mary Evans Picture Library 26; Photri 10 (top), 24; John Topham 10 (bottom); Wayland Picture Library (Tim Woodcock) 22; Zefa 8, 20, cover (top); *Cover (inset)* Paul Seheult.

Index